Millionaire Mobile Home Investor

Keith Startz

Millionaire Mobile Home Investor

keithstartz.com

Copyright © 2010 Keith Startz

CreateSpace

Self help/How to

First Edition (July, 2010)
First Printing (July, 2010)

ISBN: 978-1453662014

Keith Startz
Millionaire Mobile Home Investor

So you want to be a millionaire, you want to make $20,000.00 a month part time out of your own home. I'm writing this business report to educate you on how to make a million dollars in less than 5 years. Hello, my name is Keith Startz and I have been in the manufactured housing industry for well over a decade. I have sold and delivered over 1000 homes. I have also managed and developed several multi-million dollar sales centers while also being in charge of home finance, delivery & setup, construction, insurance & of course service.

The first thing you want to do is check with the manufactured housing institute of your state to check if a broker or dealer license is needed to sell homes within your state. For Texas you would simply keyword in Google Texas manufactured housing association and we get www.texasmha.com. Do the same for your state and you will be fine. You can also gather a great deal of information from the department of housing and community affairs.

This is a simple blueprint laid out. The heart of this deal and what makes it work is to know where to buy the mobile homes and what to pay for them. This is a confidential list and took a long time to comprise. Some of the wholesalers on the list will often sell these homes to investors - anyone who is willing to pay the asking price. The key is not to pay the asking price but to pay below wholesale and get them for as close to 30 and 40 cents on the dollar based of NADA guide pricing. The banks have these homes priced at book value. The key to getting these homes below wholesale is experience and that comes from being in the business for many year

Now here is what I would do step by step so listen closely: and pay attention. Depending upon your state your living in will determine the steps required to do what I'm about to tell you. I would first approach these financial institutions and let them know you are an investor and would like to buy some of their mobile home repos. A lot of them may say certainly some may say do you have an RBI Retailer Broker Installer license. Believe me you can go on a few investor boards related to mobile home investing and if you mention you made need a license they look at you like your crazy saying I buy all the time and have never been asked. So maybe it's just my state Texas that you need one. Here are the directions of how I would approach this new and exciting adventure you are about to embark on.

What I would do is call up a bank from the list of financial institutions and tell them your name and that you are looking at buying some mobile homes and if she/he would be kind enough to fax you a list of their repos. You will receive a list with their asking price they will never tell you their wholesale price and what it will take to win the bid.

The going wholesale price on a 16 X 80 single section home 1998-2001 in decent condition is around 10-14 grand is what you will get it for

Sometimes a little less. Now the beauty of it is you call a carpet cleaning company and have the carpet shampooed for $100,00 give the home a good cleaning and sell it for $25K as for delivery and set of the home you can work out the details with your customer. Deliveries on single section homes average about $2k to $3k depending on the distance to the home site. So do make it a rule of thumb to try and always get three bids on everything. You can start to see the potential for making big money in this business. Or simply let your customer handle the delivery and sell it for 3K less.

There are a few simple steps when selling a mobile home. You can get the forms to write up the deals from your manufactured housing association or department of housing and community affairs. They will tell you what you need for your state. It is usually 5 to 10 pages it will vary depending upon which state you reside in. There are also a few steps after the sale of the home. You need to get three bids for delivery and they will vary considerably. You need to contact an AC company and have them do the AC disconnect and rehook this will cost you around $250 to $350.00 most of the time they will just put the AC unit in the back of the home usually the utility room by the back door. Just remember to have the utilities disconnected before the delivery company comes to get the home.

It really is that simple if you want to get an RBI Retailer Broker Installer license and also have the option of selling consignment repos from large lenders like 21st mortgage who will also finance their own repos Then you will need a broker or dealers license. If you just want to buy wholesale and sell retail then you may not need a license depending upon your states requirements.

As for getting your license it is pretty simple. For Texas it is a 3-day training class no test or anything like that. You get a lot of information and a rather large manual with copies of everything you will need. Purchase memos title forms and a lot more. You have to get a bond and an insurance policy and that's about it. And no you do not need a lot or inventory to get your RBI in Texas and yes you can sell straight out of your home office.

So there you have it short and sweet. Now the math on making a million Sell three homes a month with an average $7K profit in each like the example above Multiply profit times number of sells (three) equals $21 thousand a month times 50 months equals $1,050.000.00 in less than 5 years. And even if you do just one sell a month you're still making darn good part time money from working at home. This is the real making money from home deal.

You may ask how you sell the homes, who do you market to. Just take out a small line ad in your local paper and the weekly papers. A couple of line ads in a couple of papers should do the trick. If you want to really market it heavily then I would by your papers in bulk. Go to http://www.nationwideadvertising.com/ you can buy various package deals that cover your entire state. http://www.myclassifiedads.net/ run a simple ad like 2000 Palm Harbor 16 X 80 big kitchen lots of cabinets three bedroom two bath home $24,900.00 central air Installed setup & delivery included. Just find one ad that works and simply multiply it in many papers.

Since you will be working from home a Virtual Salesman is a must have for the home business the benefits of adding an 800 number with fax on demand capabilities. Your virtual salesman works 24 hours a day and never requires time of. If a customer calls the 800 number, they can request free brochures & literature as well as floor plans. Information can be accessed 24/7 instead of 9-5 without hiring or training a single person. Before you were open 8 hours a day to service your customers now you are open 24 hours a day to get the information into the hands of your potential clients. How much more productive could your office be with a 24 hour virtual salesman which faxes out time sensitive material like house listing. Example press 2 for new home listings then enter your fax number and receive actual hard copies of floor plans, features & benefits. Foreclosures that is available in your area. Press 3 for land/home packages available. Press 4 for a credit application. The truly nice thing about having a virtual salesman is they can also receive faxes on the same 800 number people call in on. One simple number does it all.

Let's take it a step further everyone knows what a pain it is to call in for your messages and go through all the button pushing, sometimes we accidentally delete an important message that could have been a sell. Well now you can have all your voice messages delivered to your email. Then you can simply click on a message to play it. Pause it in between etc. This Virtual Salesman concept would work wonders in the home office profession especially if you are going to be a dealer.

A potential customer calls your dealership after hours and requests brochures on a certain type of home and instantly receives it by fax along with a warm sales greeting outlining the many benefits of your business. The key behind this system working is it is totally self-contained and automated. As for the 800 minutes you can buy them in bulk for as little as 4.9 cents a minute. I typically buy 1000 minutes a month which goes both ways incoming voice incoming fax outgoing fax. My favorite option with my virtual salesman is the ability to receive voice messages by email. Especially when you have 20 or 30 messages. All you have to do is click on the message and it begins to play. You can pause it and replay with the click of a button.

One of the nicest features of all is to be able to work from home without sounding like you are a small time home business. I opted to write my own script and had it professionally recorded in a studio. I even wrote and had a commercial recorded so when a client is on hold they will hear my commercial for upgrading to Hardy Panel exterior siding. I took advantage of everything my virtual salesman had to offer. Now when people call my business it sounds more like a major corporation then a one-person home business. I have my fax-on-demand setup if a customer is interested in singlewide homes press 2 and he will receive a page on my credentials and my experience in the industry, page two will be the features & benefits of the homes as well as three different floor plans. The same works for a client wanting information on doublewide homes. I also have it setup so a client can receive a list of foreclosures. And yes I did not forget the credit application or mortgage application. The client can have it faxed to them fill it out and fax it back to the same number.

Only in America, I love this country. Where else can you run a full blown dealership out of your own home by yourself and come across sounding like a million bucks? Now you may say wait a minute what about inventory and a lot to place them on. Inventory is known as flooring in the mobile home industry. That's what is so cool, I have no lot and I have no inventory, which means no overhead that I can do without. I did not need them to get my RBI license Retailer Broker Installer. I sell of floor plans and if a client really wants to see a new home in person I offer to personally take them on a FREE factory tour.

I meet them and drive them to the factory and give them a personalized tour of how the homes are built. Key point here. When you setup your business to sell new homes as well as foreclosures try and sell new homes that are actually built within your state. Fortunately I'm within 100 miles of the factory where the new homes are built. A factory tour just adds so much to the credibility of selling new homes with your business. You see I don't have a sales lot with homes on paying super high overhead. I now have a fully functioning factory with around 100 employees.

I guarantee you if you called my 800 virtual salesmen you would certainly get the feel of a large corporation. It's what people perceive to believe that counts. Belief is a powerful suggestion. Now for a break down and instructions of costs & profits associated with buying bank owned foreclosures. In Texas anyone can sell mobile homes out of their garage. The key to starting out is get to know the banks that have the foreclosure list also know as repo list. I have supplied you with a list of the best banks to work with and yes I even included those wonderful 800 numbers so it won't even cost you a dime to call them. Yes some have websites with pictures of their inventory and prices on the homes. Warnings do not pay the price you see listed, that price is for consumers, remember you are a dealer now. You pay dealer prices. Just one example you see a nice clean 16 X 80 singlewide listed at $26,000 you offer them between 10 & 14 I would not go more than 14 on any 16 X 80 singlewide. Remember you are also responsible for any back taxes and lot rent. Simply call the local tax office to get any back taxes information. If there is some back taxes on the home or back lot rent on the home use this information as ammunition to get the price down on the home.

Let's say there is $1500.00 in back taxes and $500.00 in back lot rent. Offer them $12,000.00 for the home all total you are in the home for $14,000.00 get in touch with the land owner before you buy the home and work out a deal with him to let the home stay where it's at. Offer to pay him the normal months lot rent usually $200.00 or so. Once you have all your numbers worked out and made arrangements with the landowner bid the 12K on the home. If you are not sure how much to bid on manufactured homes get yourself one of those NADA manufactured home guides. It's the same as the auto books. So you purchased your first home for $12,000.00 you have $1500.00 in back taxes and $500.00 in back lot rent. You cut a deal with the landowner for $200.00 a month to leave it there. You do not want to have to move the homes if at all possible it sucks up your profit in and around $2,000.00 a pop on average.

You want to move the home just once and that is when you sell it. And that's only if you want to get involved in moving them, which includes disconnecting utilities and the central air unit. You need a certified AC guy to disconnect the central air unit to prevent the average Joe from disconnecting it wrong and costing you some money in the tune of $1500.00 give or take a little. You do not want to get into replacing central air units. You simply need an ac disconnect & rehook after the home has been delivered and installed to where it's going. A/C disconnects & re-hooks should cost around $350.00 total you can get your appliances from Lowe's or home depot. It would be a good idea to get an account at one of the two or both. I usually always give them a new frig and stove, I pick them out, don't make the mistake of letting customers pick them out. You will end up paying for the most expensive the store offers. This can easily run in the thousands. Go the extra mile and purchase them a basic range and refrigerator. Your customers will love you.

This is exactly how you go about acquiring referrals and believe me referrals is the name of the game. Just one referral a month can be worth $7 to $10 thousand dollars simply because you cared enough to go the extra mile and add a little more personal service to your deal.

If you're really smart and want build a trophy database of clients that will help you generate a long term referral network. Simply always get their birthdays, anniversary dates. Then keep this valuable information in a secure database.

Then send them out birthday cards, anniversary gifts, and don't forget the holidays. People love and appreciate being thought of and shown a little love & affection. It's worth thousands of dollars to you; you are learning to maximize your income by simply triggering a person's emotion with a .99 cent card. Only in America, this is how to virtually guarantee fat referral network. This will generate a powerful cash flow machine. We are not talking about a few hundred dollars here were dealing in the tens of thousands.

Ok back to our original deal. We invested in a 1998 Fleetwood 16 X 80 mobile home for $12,000 We have $1500 in back taxes, $500 in back lot rent we paid an additional $200 to keep the home in its original purchased location so we wouldn't have to spend additional monies, it would normally cost to move the home. This will maximize our return on investment. We also spent about $800 at Lowes for a basic refrigerator and range. Plus we paid our electrician about $350.00 for a standard AC quick disconnect. Do not disconnect the AC unit until it's time to move the home. This will only entice your neighbors and passerby's to steal your unit.

So we are in it for a total of $15,350.00 without delivery & install. Most deliveries of 16 x 80 singlewide homes typically go for around $2,000 if delivered within a standard 50 mile radius and there are no complications. If you agreed to handle the delivery & install make sure you always get at least a minimum three bids. They will always vary wildly. Keep in mind a $2,000 bid is a very fair bid for a standard delivery and set, which includes blocked leveled and tied down to state code.

If I were new and just starting out in the business with limited knowledge and experience I would simply leave the delivery out. Just inform your client that you are not licensed and bonded to handle deliveries, if you were then they would have paid significantly more the home they just purchased from you. Just educate your client on deliveries and explain to them that it is critically important that they get a minimum of three bids even more if possible. This will ensure them of saving allot of money.

Once again let's get back to our investment on wheels. We did our homework and now know the book value of this home is $25,000 Remember the bank was asking $26,000 Typically banks will price there foreclosures around book value.

The biggest obstacle and learning curve in this industry is to have an understanding and feel for what to pay for your foreclosures. Your target number and goal is always to pay well below dealer wholesale prices.

There is no good book or easy way to get around this learning curve. The best you can possibly do it purchase the manufactured housing appraisal guide from N.A.D.A you can obtain these books online.

As you progress ever so carefully through each deal you invest in you will start to gain incredibly valuable experience worth thousands of dollars at lightning speed, I guarantee it. The reason I say this and can assure you so confidently is because if you don't it will literally cost you thousands of dollars on each and every deal.

As your skills develop and your senses sharpen for your new trade you will start to notice all you have to do is spend 10 minutes or less walking through a home to come up with a fair price to pay for your home of choice that will of course always be in your favor.

Whatever you do don't get excited and let your emotions get involved if you do you are setting yourself up for a painful lesson that could easily cripple or hurt your business for a couple of months and leave you scarred from a single deal. Believe me you won't be able to survive many of these trails of life.

Keith Startz

Now back to our Mobile Home Repo. We have a total of $15,350.00 into this deal. Our book value is $25,000.00 do not get greedy there will always be plenty more to flip and make money from. Your objective should be to flip it and turn it as quickly as possible. Let's sell it quick for an easy $22K which is far less then what all the mobile home dealers in town are asking for the same home. They are all asking for $25K or more. We will sell for $22K and close the customer contacting him as being responsible for his own delivery, which he is happy to pay because you just convinced him of how much money he is saving by getting his own bids and taking the middle man out of the equation which of course saves him big money or so he thinks. The truth is we want to maximize or profit and limit our risk at every corner of the deal.

Selling at a quick short $22K you should unload it within a few weeks which will net you a quick $6650.00 in pure profit. Not bad for a little leg work and a round of easy paper work. Sure you had to speak with a few people and show the home a couple of time but all easy money and there is allot more where that came from I can assure you.

The way I calculate and work my numbers is by keeping it simple and using a basic rule to go by. It's your business now so set your own numbers as you wish. I like to keep the profit in my singlewides at a minimum $5,000.00 and my doublewides no less than $7500.00 With these numbers I will turn more home and keep feeding my machine and getting it nice and fat for the winter. Your business will slow down a little, not much but a little during

November & December. So make sure you turned at least ten homes by then for the year. That way you should be nice and fat with a little extra cash. Remember we are basing this on a part time gig at this point, don't give up your day job right away, and prove yourself first. Also try and score at least two or three jumbos a year more if possible. These are your super fat cats so to speak and will instantly put a huge smile on your face. Tag and bag one the larger of the breed which are the major doublewides. The bigger the better and the more profit. Usually the 70 and 80 footers will rain in the most cash. It's not on usually to pay only $25K for a 28X80 and turn around and flip it in less than a month for $56K to 58K. If you want a super fine easy ride then set your mobile business to cruise control and target the big guns only. Flip two or three a year for around 25K each in profit. Or set some goals and take a more aggressive approach and go after an early retirement shoot for one a month at 25K a pop which will give you a smooth $300K a year.

Now let's do something nice and give back to our community we live in. Let's reduce the profit we make on each home by 5K this way we can accelerate the number of homes we sale per month. This will also ensure quick and easy sales on every unit we turn. You will find that you will sleep better and live a happier life. The reason behind this is quite simple ever time you sell a home you make 20K which is a great day. This in turn puts a big smile on your face and you instantly feel successful and happy. This will lead you into the life drams are made of major security and happiness. Your wife is now happy and proud of you and so are your kids. What else can a person possibly want. You are now leaving the dream.

Let's go for an easy $20K profit per home. With these discount prices you are giving your homes away for $10,000.00 less than any dealer in town; no one can come close or touch your super discount fire sale prices. The bonus that lies within this magic is everyone you sell a home to will love you and be grateful to you. You just gave them the deal of a lifetime.

This will help cut down on the guilt you will start to feel because you are making more money in one day then most people make in six months. Just remember you are helping people you are selling your homes at wholesale prices while your competitors the majors, the dealers are scalping people by selling the same home as you for $10,000.00 more you are. You will be looked upon by your community as a hero. Now doesn't that make you feel better about all that money you're making of from each sale?

Ok enough with the selling structure and the mechanics of the sale. Show me the money; I want to know how to generate one million dollars. You asked for it you got, here is how it's done. Calculate the $20K profit you make of each large doublewide. All you have to do is sell 50 of them and you're a millionaire. The question is simply how aggressive are you, do you want to become a millionaire in 5 years or 10 years. Still not quite enough for you,

you want more one million just isn't enough you now see the true potential and earning power this cash machine is capable of generating. You know that all you have to do is tweak it just a little bit here and there and throw in some mental conditioning and you will have then created the first mobile home foreclosure wealth building machine. This key of knowledge that you have just released and unlocked by taking action and believing in yourself has generated your very own blue print to success and happiness by designing a safe and secure road map to becoming a multi-millionaire.

Here is the secret to making your first million within the first few years of launching your business. All you have to do is run a simple classified ad in the sales help wanted section in your local paper. Remember always keep it simple. Here is your ad. "Experienced Sales people needed. Flex hours earn 30% selling homes.

The beauty of this model is how it works. You hire two or three or as many as you like, you're the boss. You don't pay them a penny unless they sell a home. Then you only pay them when the deal is completely 100% finished and your pure profit is setting in your bank account. Then and only then you cut them their check for a flat 30% of the net profit from their sale. You 1099 them so you cut down on your paper work and don't have to mess with their taxes. This way they must tax themselves at the end of the year and it's not your problem. Remember always keep it clean and simply.

Another beauty you get when using this system. They must use their own vehicle, pay for their own gas they are completely independent and on their own, they pay all their own expenses. You only pay them based on their performance. They are responsible for setting their own appointments; Set the rules up front you are the boss and they are responsible for selling and closing at least one home every month, if they fell to sell a home within a three month or go 90 days straight without a sale they will be released or terminated you choose the language you use. You should write out a contract that's spells out in plain English exactly what you expect from your sales people. In return you must spell out on the same contract what you will do for them in return for their loyalty and dedication. How you will support them and always be available for them when they need you. Offer a $1,000.00 cash bonus anytime one of your consultants sales and closes two homes within the same month.

Also they sale their first home get them some business cards from the local print shop. You want to give them dignity and build confidence and pride into your people. Help develop and sharpen their skills constantly you do this by building them up with positive affirmations. You want to build and develop a bond between you and your team, you want loyalty and long term employees that you can count on that are well trained and will be with you for as long as it takes you to reach your goals, whatever that may be. Once your new system is in place and functioning smoothly you are then set on auto pilot, sit back relax, collect checks from your team and make deposits into bank and watch your wealth begin to explode.

You must have one single unbreakable rule that must be followed and enforced at all cost. Every contact written will include a purchase memo on this purchase you must make certain that one sentence, just a couple of words but these words are critically important. Have them write on the contract purchase memo "Contingent upon General Managers Approval" That's your loop hole out of the deal in case something go's wrong for any reason that may come up. You always set make sure you have the advantage and the upper hand and control in all situations you encounter in life, especially your business.

Remember you play the part when in contact with the client that you are the General Manager, you don't want them to know you are the owner if you do allow them to know that you are setting yourself up for extra problems and difficulties that will come up from time to time that can easily be avoided by simple playing it cool and keeping a low profile. Remember this isn't a power trip do not slip into that idiotic behavior. If you do then simple kiss your dreams good bye. You will not succeed, you will fail. You have a clear purpose in mind and life and have a blue print to millions, stay focused and on the correct path and stick to the rules you have written in the beginning for yourself to keep you on track and don't get a big head either.

Once a little money starts coming in furnish all your sales people with new cell phones on a single business account that you pay and control. You are also responsible for driving the sales and generating the leads for your sales people to follow and track down sale and close. You had better keep good leader adds running at all times in many different papers, daily and weeklies. You must keep these ads fresh and rotate them out at least once every month, I prefer every three weeks. Stick with the plan and never ever drift away from it. Have these ads running directly to each of your sales peoples cell phones. That way they are on call 24/7 and can't miss a call a lead. Remember these leads can be worth $20K a piece, missing just one can be catastrophic

Let's run a few numbers. The most I have made in one month with a couple of sells people was a little over $100,000.00 the most I have ever made on a single deal was $37,000.00 which was a 32 X 80 Palm Harbor I sold for $70,000.00. The same Palm Harbor sells new for close to $120K so I saved my clients $50,000 and made myself $37,000. It was a win/win situation for both of us. The really weird thing about sells is the customers you make the most money on seem to always be the happiest ones. The ones you make the least amount on are always complaining. That's just how it seems to work.

Here are a few more rules to follow when inspecting homes. Plywood flooring is always best. Nova deck & particleboard is low grade but will do just fine because you are going to find it in most of the homes you inspect and sell. Stay away from homes that have polybutelene plumbing as it was in a major class action law suit. When doing a walk through make sure the floors are solid and there are no soft spots. Always check the ceiling closely for any water spots from leakage. Always look under the cabinets and open all drawers and make sure they have roller guides. Also check and make sure the water heater is still in the home. People will pack everything off including the light bulbs and doorknobs. Target vinyl sided exterior homes over metal exterior homes. Always go after composition shingle roofs over metal roofs. Go with hardboard siding over metal siding. I am speaking from experience and telling you want sells best and what people prefer and are looking for.

The secret key that you must find to make this blue print that I have just shared with you work is knowledge which you will only be able to gain through experience which requires time and dedication on your part. That is the true key that is blended and becomes one with your own burning desire that you must have never give up and succeed at all cost failure is not an option and will lead only to certain death.

Vanderbilt   865-380-3523   www.vmfrepos.com
Origen Financial 800-492-1874 www.ofllc.com
21st   Mortgage   800-955-0021
www.21stMortgage.com Triad Financial 904-223-1111 www.triadfs.com US Bank 858-720-7116
Popular   Housing   Services   724-873-3543
www.tammac.com   www.origenhomes.com
www.21strepos.com   www.vmfrepos.com

Keith Startz

GREENTREE REPOS 800-643-0202 www.gtservicing.com ALABAMA 800-940-3581 ARIZONA 800-328-8214 ARKANSAS 800-576-1021 CALIFORNIA 800-365-0089 COLORADO 800-525-8799 FLORIDA 800-874-1159 GEORGIA 800-874-1159 IDAHO 800-392-4276 INDIANA 800-532-7768 MICHIGAN 800-444-1968 MINNESOTA 877-245-6267 MISSISSIPPI 800-874-0793 MISSOURI 800-392-4276 MONTANA 800-548-2632 NEVADA 800-365-0089 NEW HAMPSHIRE 800-992-1018 OHIO 800-686-6600 OKLAHOMA 800-333-4482 OREGON 800-562-2510 SOUTH CAROLINA 800-922-0010 TENNESSEE 800-234-7101 TEXAS 800-772-5361 TEXAS 800-292-7413 VIRGINIA 800-669-2178 VIRGINIA 800-234-7101 WASHINGTON 800-562-2510 WISCONSIN 877-245-6267 CHASE BANK REPOS WESTERN U. S. 888-667-9133 EASTERN U. S. 800-225-6761

Mobile Home Buyers Guide

Hello, my name is Keith Startz and I have been in the manufactured housing industry for over 20 years. I have sold and delivered over 5000 homes. I have also managed and developed several multi-million dollar sales centers while also being in charge of home finance, delivery & setup, construction, insurance & of course service.

Buying a home may be the most expensive purchase you will ever make. A manufactured home may be an appealing option for you. These homes come in a variety of styles, sizes, and floor plans, and range in price from about $15,000 to more than $100,000, without land. Manufactured homes can be installed on your own land, in a rental community, or in a planned subdivision.

The affordability of manufactured housing is mainly attributable to the efficiencies of the factory process. The controlled environment and assembly line techniques remove many of the problems of the site-built sector, such as poor weather, theft, vandalism and damage to building products and materials stored on site. Also, factory employees are trained, scheduled and managed by one employer, as opposed to the system of contracted labor in the site-built sector.

Manufactured home producers also benefit from the economies of scale, which result from being able to purchase large quantities of building materials and products. As a result they are able to negotiate the lowest possible price for items that are invariably more expensive in a site-built house.

The factory process builds the home from the "inside out," which results in ease of installation for interior walls and plumbing and electrical systems. The house and materials on an assembly line travel to the workers, with scaffolds, tools and materials within easy reach. Computer-assisted design (CAD) programs also offer speed and flexibility for manufacturers.

Today's manufactured homes come with many "standard" features that you would find in a site-built home. Many floor plans are available that range from the basic models to more elaborate designs with living and dining rooms with vaulted ceilings, fully-equipped modern kitchens, comfortable bedrooms with walk-in closets, and bathrooms with recessed bathtubs and whirlpools.

You may also select from a variety of exterior designs, including metallic, vinyl, wood, or hardboard. You also may select such design features as a bay window, a gable front, or a pitched roof with shingle. Awnings, enclosures around the crawl space, patio covers, decks, and steps are also available at additional costs.

The History of the Manufactured Home
Humble beginnings, grand endings.

The manufactured home of today is an evolution of style and amenities that has its roots in a history of answering the American public's demand for quality housing at an exceptional value.

In the 1920s, "trailer coaches" were built to serve the American traveler who wanted the ability, when vacationing, of having a ready-made place to sleep at a campsite. During World War II, these temporary dwellings were used to house factory workers who came from miles around to aid in the war effort.

When the war ended, veterans came home to find affordable housing in short supply. The industry answered this call by building homes that were large enough to house a veteran and his family. However, these homes could still be moved from one location to another to provide the mobility that the family desired.

In the 1960s, American consumers wanted even more out of the industry. The demand was for bigger trailers with more amenities and the new appliances that were rapidly coming on the market. And still, it had to be mobile. History buffs may remember Lucille Ball in the movie, "The Long, Long Trailer."

From this demand was born the mobile home. Mobile homes were bigger in size, nicer in appearance and met the needs of prospective young American homeowners.

In 1974, Congress passed the National Mobile Home Construction and Safety Standards Act, also known as the HUD Code. This watershed legislation made mobile homes the only form of private and single-family building subject to federal regulation. Even site-built homes did not enjoy such strict regulation. These regulations, which became effective in June of 1976, preempted any existing state or local construction and safety codes applying to the product.

The effect of federal regulation was to more clearly define mobile homes as buildings, rather than vehicles. The Housing Act of 1980 adopted this change officially, mandating the use of "manufactured housing" (factory-built homes) to replace "mobile homes" in all federal law and literature for homes built since 1976.

The manufactured home you see today is truly a home and it bears little resemblance to its 'tin-box' predecessor, the trailer. Often, you may not even recognize a manufactured home - so close is it in design and structure to its site-built counterpart. Thanks to sophisticated production processes and the demands of the consumer, manufactured homes have become a model of efficiency, affordability, and innovative design options.

Mobile Home Myths and Reality
Myth: There is a traditional perception that manufactured housing is more vulnerable to fire than other forms of single-family housing.

Reality: The fact is that manufactured homes are no more prone to fire than homes built on site, according to an annual report released by the Oklahoma State Fire Marshall's office.

Similar studies have echoed the above statement made by the Foremost Insurance Company. A national fire safety study conducted by the Foremost Insurance Company shows that site-built homes are more than twice more likely to experience a fire than manufactured homes. According to this study, the number of home fires is 17 per 1,000 for site-built homes, while only eight per 1,000 for manufactured homes.

Storm Safety

Myth: Manufactured homes are particularly vulnerable to the destructive force of strong winds and tornadoes. Manufactured homes seem to attract tornadoes.

Reality: Hurricane Andrew struck the southern tip of Florida and the Gulf Coast regions of Louisiana in late August 1992 with devastating winds in excess of 150 miles-per-hour. The third strongest hurricane ever to strike the United States, Andrew was designated a Category 4. Thousands of homes, both site built and manufactured, suffered extensive damage and destruction from the force of the storm.

There is no meteorological or scientific basis to thinking that manufactured homes attract tornadoes. The reality is one of coincidence: most manufactured homes are located in rural and suburban locations, where meteorological conditions favor the creation of tornadoes.

Energy Efficiency
Myth: Manufactured homes are less energy efficient than site-built homes.

Reality: On October 24, 1994 a new minimum energy conversation standard became effective. The new energy standards are resulting in lower monthly energy bills; a factor industry officials say will enhance the affordability of manufactured housing and, perhaps, improve mortgage underwriting terms. Improved home ventilation standards have also been adopted in conjunction with the energy standards, a step that will improve indoor air quality and condensation control in manufactured homes.

The new standards rely on computer modeling to identify the optimum cost-effective conservation level for a home located in any one of three regions in the nation. In developing the standards, the U.S. Department of Housing and Urban Development followed Congress mandate to establish standards that "minimize the sum of construction and operating costs" over the life of the home. This emphasis on "lifecycle" energy costs is unique among national energy standards.

Home Appreciation
Myth: Manufactured homes do not appreciate in value like other forms of housing. Instead, manufactured homes depreciate in market value, similar to the way automobiles lose value each day.

Reality: While there is no one easy answer, recent data seems to suggest that manufactured homes can appreciate just like other forms of housing.

Datacomp Appraisal Systems recently completed a study that looked at 185 manufactured homes in Michigan, comparing the average sale price when new to the average resale price several years later. The study found the average value of the home had increased by $190, from $26,422 new to $26,612 used. This average figure is misleading, in that 97 of the homes increased in value by an average of $2,985, while the remaining 88 decreased in value by an average of $2,822.

The only accurate conclusion is that some homes appreciate and some don't. Based on an analysis of 88,000 actual sales, Datacomp found that there are specific reasons why some homes appreciate while other depreciate. These reasons include:

The housing market, in which the home is located, will have a significant impact on the future value of the home.
The community, in which the home is located, has a similarly significant impact on the home's future value.
The initial price paid for the home.
The age of the home.
The inflation rate.

The availability and cost of community sites, which reflects the supply and demand influences on the home's value.

The extent of an organized resale network, where an organized network will usually result in homes selling for a higher price than in markets without such an organized network.

tithe areciation in value of manufactured homes comes back to the old real estate axiom -- location, location, location. When properly sited and maintained, manufactured homes will appreciate at the same rate as other homes in surrounding neighborhoods.

Life of Manufactured Homes

Myth: Manufactured homes are not built as well as other forms of housing. Manufactured homes do not last as long as site-built homes.

Reality: Manufactured homes are built with virtually the same construction materials and techniques as site-built homes. The only difference is that manufactured homes are built in a factory environment, where building materials are protected from weather damage and vandalism. Manufactured homes are built to the federal Manufactured Home Construction and Safety Standards; better known as the HUD Code, which is administered by the U.S. Department of Housing and Urban Development (HUD).

THE HUD Code

Just as site built homes are constructed according to a specific building code to ensure proper design and safety, today's manufactured homes are constructed in accordance with the HUD Code. The United States Congress laid the foundation for the HUD Code in the National Manufactured Housing Construction and Safety Standards Act of 1974, which was enacted because of three inter-related reasons:

The interstate shipment of homes from the plant to the retailer to the home site meant that the manufacturer - prior to the advent of the HUD Code - ordinarily did not know in advance which code would apply;

States were not able to effectively and uniformly regulate manufactured home construction and safety issues; and

Congress wished to preserve access

to affordable
housing for middle
and lower income
families.

In its legislation, Congress directed the Secretary of
the U.S. Department of Housing and Urban
Development (HUD) to establish appropriate
manufactured home construction and safety
standards that "...meet the highest standards of
protection, taking into account existing state and
local laws relating to manufactured home safety and
construction."

Every HUD Code manufactured home is built in a
factory, under controlled conditions, and has a
special label affixed on the exterior of the home
indicating that the home has been designed,
constructed, tested and inspected to comply with the
stringent federal standards set forth in the code. No
manufactured home may be shipped from the
factory unless it complies with the HUD Code and
is released for shipment by an independent third
party inspector certified by HUD.

The HUD Code is unique since it is specifically
designed for compatibility with the factory
production process. Performance standards for
heating, plumbing, air conditioning, thermal and
electrical systems are set in the code. In addition,
performance requirements are established for
structural design, construction, fire safety, energy
efficiency, and transportation from the factory to the

customer's home site. Manufactured homes are constructed with virtually the same materials used in site-built homes. However, in contrast to traditional site-building techniques, manufactured homes have the advantage of using engineered design applications and the most cost-efficient assembly-line techniques to produce a quality home at a much lower cost per square foot. To ensure quality, both HUD and its monitoring contractor monitor the design and construction of the home. The familiar red seal (the certification label) attached to the exterior of a manufactured home indicates that it has undergone and passed perhaps the most thorough inspection process in the home building industry.

Is the HUD Code less stringent than state or local building codes?
Although the HUD Code is more performance-based while model codes, such as the CABO One-and-Two Family Dwelling Code, used by many state and local jurisdictions to regulate site-built housing tend to be more prescriptive, independent analyses and comparisons of the HUD and CABO Codes generally come to the conclusion that they are comparable in nature. A 1997 comparison study of the HUD and CABO Codes by the University of Illinois Architecture-Building Research Council stated:

There are many similarities in these codes, along with minor differences of slight consequence and some differences of notable consequence. On balance, the codes are comparable.

While some areas of the CABO code are deemed "more restrictive" than the HUD Code in the University of Illinois study, there are also areas where the HUD Code is deemed more restrictive than the CABO Code, such as in ventilation, flame spread, structural loads, window construction, vapor retarders and service wiring.

While some believe the HUD Code is solely responsible for the affordable nature of manufactured housing, the National Association of Home Builders Research Center, in a report prepared for HUD, concluded that:

...the net cumulative effect of the differences between the two codes is more likely on the order of hundreds of dollars, rather than thousands of dollars per unit.

Site Preparation, Transportation, Installation, and Inspection

Before your home is installed, make sure the site has been properly prepared. Careful attention to the following details will help ensure satisfaction with your home for years to come. Your retailer can provide you with valuable guidance and assistance.

Site Preparation

If you're having the home installed on your own land, you may be responsible for site preparation.

But it's also a good idea to have your retailer or installer inspect the site.

Here's a site preparation checklist:

The delivery truck must be able to reach the site.

The site must be as level as possible.

The area where the home will sit must be clear of trees, rocks, and other debris.

The soil must be graded and sloped away from the home for water runoff.

Fill soil must be compacted to prevent the foundation from sinking or shifting.

While you may be able to do some of the site preparation, most tasks, such as grading and compacting soil, require professional expertise. Otherwise, you could do damage to your home that's not covered by the warranty.

Delivery

In most instances, your home will be transported from the factory to the retail sales center. There, your retailer will inspect it. Any damage done to the home in transit will be repaired before it is delivered to your home site.

If damage occurs on the way from the retailer to your site, the transporter is usually held responsible. Therefore, make sure you check for damage before the home leaves the sales center and again when your home arrives at the site. If you find any damage, report it to the transporter immediately.

Before you finalize arrangements to buy and transport a home, make sure you have a written warranty from the transporter. Otherwise, if damage occurs during delivery, you could have a difficult time getting no-cost repairs.

Installation

Manufacturers must provide instructions for proper home installation. Usually, the retailer will install your home or use a contractor. Typically, the price of your home includes installation. You should get a written explanation of the installation services from your retailer. Be sure to read your contract before you sign. If installation isn't included, you may have to hire a professional. Ask your retailer for recommendations.

Whether the retailer or a contractor installs your home, follow these guidelines listed below. They will help you understand what you're paying for and how to check that the work has been done properly. You'll also better understand your warranty protections.

Get written proof of the installers qualifications. State law may require this.

Ask if there is a written warranty for installation. If not, have the contractor put in writing any promises or claims regarding the installation.

Ask the contractor to explain the installation process; have it written into the agreement.

Make sure the following six steps for installation are included in a written itemized list before you sign the purchase contract.

1. Transporting Your Home

The manufacturer is usually responsible for transporting the home from the factory to the retailer. The retailer or its transporter is usually responsible for delivering the home to your site. However, if roads are inadequate or obstacles make delivery difficult, your retailer may not be able to accept responsibility for delivery. Have the transporter check out the route beforehand to avoid problems.

2. Building a Foundation

Your home must have a foundation. In addition to following the manufacturer's instructions and complying with local codes, ask the institution financing your home or your rental community if they have special requirements. The Federal Housing Administration (FHA), Veterans Administration (VA), and the Rural Housing Service (RHS) also have special foundation requirements for homes they finance. Remind your retailer of the kind of financing you're using so that all applicable requirements will be met.

If you place your home on your own property, you can choose from a number of foundation types: concrete block, metal or treated wood piers; a concrete slab; or a full basement. A professional installer will know which local building codes apply. Ask the installer to obtain required building permits and inspections.

3. Leveling Your Home

It's critical that your home be leveled to meet the manufacturer's installation instructions. Otherwise, your home's weight will be unevenly distributed. This can cause floors and walls to buckle and prevent doors and windows from opening and closing smoothly. While the manufacturer's warranty won't cover repairs resulting from improper leveling, a written warranty from the installer may.

Insist on a walk-through before the installer leaves. Check for signs that your home may not be level.

Because some foundation supports may settle unevenly, it's important to periodically check that your home stays level. The first check should be done 60 to 90 days after installation, and then once every year.

4. Securing Your Home to the Foundation

To help minimize damage from high winds and earthquakes, your home should be anchored to the ground or concrete footers. Anchoring must comply with the manufacturer's instructions or as required by local codes. This is not a "do-it-yourself" project. Ask your retailer for more information.

5. Finishing Your Home

Your home may need finishing work, such as an enclosure around the crawl space. The enclosure must provide adequate ventilation openings at all four corners of the home. If you have a multisection home, finishing work may include molding and joining carpet on the interior, and siding and roofing work on the exterior.

6. Connecting Utilities

Installation should include connections to water, electricity, gas, and sewer. If connections aren't included in the installation price, you'll have to contract for them separately. Your retailer can help you with the arrangements, or you can contact local authorities for more information.

Additions and Alterations to Your Home

Once your home has left the factory, the HUD Code does not include provisions for additions and alterations. Such modifications may jeopardize your home warranty. They may also create malfunctions or an unsafe home. An approved addition should be a freestanding structure that meets local building codes; you may need a permit. Contact your manufacturer, the state agency that oversees manufactured housing in your state, the U.S. Department of Housing and Urban Development, or local building officials for more information.

Home Inspection

Conduct an organized inspection before you move in. Move from the exterior to the interior, carefully checking each room. Many manufacturers provide a checklist in the owner's manual. Fill it out, date it, include additional items that need servicing and promptly return it to the manufacturer. Keep copies for yourself. A delay could jeopardize your warranty.

The Manufacturer's Warranty

Warranty coverage varies among manufacturers. Retailers must make copies of warranties offered on the homes they sell available for you to review and read before you buy a home. Read them and compare coverage. The following questions may help you in doing this.

What coverage comes with the home? You may get warranties from the home manufacturer, the retailer, the transporter, the installer, and the appliance manufacturer.

What components and what types of problems do each warranty cover? What's not covered?
Does the manufacturer's written warranty cover transportation and installation? If not, are they covered by other written warranties?
How long do the warranties last?
How do I get warranty service? Who will provide it? Where will it be performed?
Are extended warranties available from the manufacturer? If so, what do they cover and cost?
Manufacturer warranties generally cover substantial defects in the following areas:
Workmanship in the structure;
Factory-installed plumbing, heating, and electrical systems; and

Factory-installed appliances, which may also be covered by separate appliance manufacturer warranties.

Manufacturer warranties DO NOT cover:

Improper installation and maintenance;

Accidents;

Owner negligence;

Unauthorized repairs; or

Normal wear and aging.

Make sure the person who performs the installation follows the manufacturer's installation instructions. Also ensure that the manufacturer's maintenance and repair instructions (contained in the consumer/homeowner's manual) are followed to keep your warranty in effect. While your retailer will perform most warranty service, the manufacturer is responsible for making sure repairs are done and completed in a timely manner.

Implied Warranties

In addition to written warranties, you may be protected by certain "implied warranties." An implied warranty is an unspoken, unwritten promise that a product is fit to be sold and used for its intended purpose. For example, a manufactured home should be fit to be sold and lived in. Implied warranties protect you even if the manufacturer or retailer offers no written warranty. Most states allow sales that exclude implied warranties ("as is" sales). However, some states do not allow sellers to exclude or limit implied warranties. Check with

Keith Startz

your state or local consumer protection officials to learn more about implied warranty protections. If you're buying a previously-owned home, ask if it's being sold with a warranty or "as is" with no written or implied warranty.

The Retailer's Warranty
A retailer may offer a warranty on a home. Ask to see the retailer's warranty in writing before buying a home. While retailer warranties vary, they typically include:

The terms of the warranty;
What you must do to keep the warranty in effect;
What you can reasonably expect from the retailer; and
That the home has been installed according to manufacturer installation instructions and local regulations.
Retailer warranties do not cover problems that arise from:
Owner negligence;
Failure by the owner to provide notice for service; and
Unauthorized repairs.

Appliance Warranties
Your home appliances also have warranties. They may come with the use and care manuals from the appliance manufacturer or be included in the home manufacturer's warranty, as required in some states. You have the right to review copies of all

warranties before you buy a home. It's a good idea to do so, and to compare coverage.

Carefully read your warranties. Note their length and terms. In most cases, you'll get service from a local appliance service center. However, if warranty service isn't available, contact your retailer for guidance.

PLACING YOUR HOME
PLACING YOUR HOME ON YOUR OWN LAND or IN A RENTAL COMMUNITY

If you own or plan to buy land for your manufactured home, there are several matters you should consider.

Zoning

In cities and suburban areas, and in some semi rural areas, you may face zoning requirements that must be met. In certain areas, there may be a prohibition against manufactured homes, or certain requirements regarding their size and exterior appearance. You can find out if there are any restrictions or requirements by contacting the local community's planning and land use department. Consult your local telephone directory for the office nearest you.

Restrictive Covenants

Restrictive covenants are limitations in property deeds that control how you can use the land. These may include a requirement that homes be a certain size or a prohibition that lands not be used for certain purposes. The title search, conducted when you buy the land, may reveal information about such restrictions. Sometimes, however, the restrictions are described in ways that are difficult to understand. You may want to check with an experienced real estate attorney to see if there are any restrictive covenants that would keep you from placing your home on the land you are considering.

Utilities
Although a manufactured home comes complete with plumbing, electrical, and heating systems, it must, like all homes, be connected to electrical, water, and sewerage facilities. If your site is in a well-developed area, all necessary utilities may be available, subject to connection charges. Find out exactly what utilities are available and how much it will cost to connect your home to all utility sources. Contact your local public utilities division for information about utility services in your area.

Make sure the applicable zoning laws and the deed on your land will allow a manufactured home to be placed there. There are a number of important questions to consider when placing your manufactured home in a rental community.

Electrical Facilities
Electricity is usually available in all areas. But if the area where you plan to live does not have ready access to electric power, connection could be quite expensive. Check with the local power company to find out whether electricity is readily accessible.

Water Facilities

In many locations, there may not be local government-supplied water lines. If there is no water, you may have to drill a well. Do not assume that all drilling will provide water. Check with a local well-drilling company about costs and whether success is guaranteed. Also, check with local health authorities to make certain there are no problems with the quality of the water in the area.

Sewerage Facilities

Many areas still rely on septic tank systems instead of a city or county sanitary sewerage system. If you cannot connect your home to a sewerage system, you must check with local authorities about installing a septic tank. Properly installed septic systems can work quite well. But sometimes they cannot be used; for example, where the soft is not able to absorb the discharged waste. For more information, contact the local health department or the office responsible for granting building permits.

PLACING YOUR HOME IN A RENTAL COMMUNITY

You may want to place your home on a leased site in a community especially planned for manufactured housing. Placing your home in such a community usually involves fewer practical problems.

If you are interested in a rental community, visit the ones in the area where you wish to live. In addition, some manufactured home retailers may operate their own rental communities, so you may wish to ask the retailer for information and advice about them. Find out what each community offers and the differences among them, including the financial aspects, such as rental and installation costs and any miscellaneous service charges.

There also are several questions you will want to ask before deciding upon a particular rental community.
Is a written lease required and, if so, for how long?

What are the charges for utility connections or other services?

Do the community's rules require that it be responsible for installing your home, or can you let your retailer do the job?

What charges will be made for installation? Who will be responsible for ground maintenance, snow removal, refuse collection, street maintenance, and mail?

What are the community's rules and regulations? For example, are pets prohibited? Can you accept and live with such rules?

Are there any special requirements or restrictions when you sell your home?

Are there any provisions to protect you if the owner of the manufactured home community where you lease your home site sells the property for another purpose? If you must move because of a sale, will the owner help with relocation expenses, or is private or public assistance available?

THE INSPECTION SYSTEM FOR MANUFACTURED HOMES

It can generally be acknowledged that a building code is only as good as the enforcement system that accompanies it. The manufactured home enforcement program required by the U.S. Department of Housing and Urban Development (HUD) is a thorough and efficient system designed specifically for the factory production environment. Because the factory pace differs from that of the construction site, the manufactured home enforcement system is necessarily different, too. However, the goal in both cases is the same - to ensure the highest degree of safety in the design and construction of the home. The HUD enforcement system relies on a cooperative federal/state program to ensure compliance with the Federal Manufactured Home Construction and Safety Standards (the HUD Code). The Department of Housing and Urban Development enforces the HUD Code through its monitoring contractor. Uniformity and consistency can be maintained better in the HUD enforcement system because of two key factors. First, the inspections take place in the factory and follow behind the manufacturer's own in-plant inspection and quality assurance teams. This allows for more thoroughness, since time is spent inspecting homes rather than traveling to inspection sites. Efficiency is increased because travel time is limited and necessary paperwork is minimized. Second, consistency is maintained because fewer people inspect more homes. The enforcement procedure is much less susceptible to individual interpretations, as would be the case with on-site inspections in every jurisdiction across the country.

Inspection Starts before Production Starts

The HUD enforcement system begins with oversight by the Design Approval Primary Inspection Agency (DAPIA). The DAPIA (a third party inspection agency) must: approve the engineering design of the home; approve the manufacturer's quality assurance manual for its plant; and coordinate with the other third-party inspection agency, known as the IPIA. The Production Inspection Primary Inspection Agency (IPIA) has the responsibility to make sure the production facility programs and procedures are in accordance with the DAPIA approved quality assurance manual; and, it conducts inspections of homes produced in the factory to assure conformance with the approved design. Three interesting notes: 1) every home is inspected during at least one stage of production; 2) in the course of each plant visit, the IPIA makes a complete inspection of every phase of production and every visible part of each home in production; and 3) when a new plant is opened by the manufacturer, the first home built according to approved plans is inspected 100 percent - every step in the building process undergoes close scrutiny by the inspection agency. Along with this, the audit inspection teams of HUD's monitoring contractors conduct representative inspections as a check on the performance of the third party inspection agents and the manufacturer.

Keep in mind that all this is in addition to the inspections carried out by the manufacturers own foremen and its quality assurance inspectors.

Certification Assures the Homebuyer
Before leaving the factory, each home must have a numbered certification label affixed to the exterior of each section of the home. This label certifies to the homebuyer that the home has been inspected in accordance with the HUD enforcement procedures and that it complies with the HUD building code. Only when all inspection parties are satisfied that the home complies with the code will the certification label be affixed to the home. A consumer seeing the home for the first time will have the assurance that the home has been thoroughly tested and inspected from the design stage through final construction and found to be built according to the approved design.

CONSUMER SATISFACTION

According to a study by the Foremost Insurance Company, 88 percent of manufactured homeowners report satisfaction with their housing choice. Likewise, a most recent Owens Corning study, conducted by National Family Opinion, found that 93 percent of manufactured home owners are satisfied with their housing choice.

Make a Plan and Get Pre-Qualified.

Armed with the following when applying for a loan will make the process a lot less stressful and make it seem like a breeze.

Full Names and Social Security numbers of all.
Your home address, including zip code, for the last 24 months.
If you were renting, a copy of the lease, the landlords name and address, and monthly payments
If you are military a copy of your orders. If you living in leased or base housing a letter from the housing office stating you occupied quarters
A list of all account numbers, current balances, and complete bank address for all checking, savings, and credit union accounts
Copies of your last three months checking, savings, and retirement account statements
List all retirement fund information, including serial numbers of savings bonds, stocks, and similar assets. Provide copies of Award Letters
Copies of most recent investment account statements

If you are obligated to pay alimony, child support, or separate maintenance, bring a copy of the recorded divorce decree and/or maintenance agreement

For VA or FHA/VET loans, you will need to provide your VA Certificate of Eligibility. If you have not obtained the Certificate of Eligibility it is wise to immediately apply for it now. This will save time and prevent a lot of stress

Name and complete address and phone number of employers (for all applicants) for the last 24 months

Most recent pay stubs covering one full month and Year To Date for all applicants or a copy of your last 3 pay stubs

For military members, you will need a Statement of Service from your Commander

Last two years W-2 forms for all applicants

If you are using Child Support it is always helpful if you have a statement from the Court that disburses the payments. Writing to the Court and asking for a copy of past payments made or copies of checks you received can obtain this. If this is not available, copies of your bank statements showing regular deposits

You will also need a copy of the Decree that establishes the Child Support in the current amount. It is also wise to have a copy of the Divorce Decree

If you are unable to provide the required documentation, your lender, under the Alternate Documentation Program, will tell you what type of document can replace the required document.

Credit Explained

Creditworthiness of Borrowers

Generally, with any lender, the degree of financial risk involved is the overriding concern when considering whether to approve a loan. To weight that risk, lenders consider two primary factors:

The borrower's ability and willingness to repay the mortgage debt, and
The appraised market value of the mortgaged property. Giving full consideration to both factors helps ensure the borrower is a good credit risk.

To further minimize the lender's financial risk, the loan is also secured by the home as collateral. Among the primary criteria lenders use to evaluate a borrower's creditworthiness are:

INCOME from salary or other sources must be stable and verifiable, have a history or track record and be likely to continue in the future. Applicants with frequent or recent job changes must provide sufficient, justifiable explanations. Income derived from sources other than employment generally takes extra time and effort for the lender to confirm. Frequently, the lender may request that federal income tax returns from previous years or a business's financial statement and balance sheet be submitted.

The applicant's willingness to repay the loan in a timely manner is a vital consideration in approving a loan. A satisfactory record of mortgage payments on previously owned real estate or rental payments is important.

To review the applicant's full credit history, lenders obtain a standard factual data credit report from the Credit Bureau. Late payments, past-due accounts, collections, judgments and bankruptcies reflect irresponsibility toward repaying debt and must be explained fully by the borrower. Other alternative credit sources may be researched if a credit history report isn't available.

ASSETS

To qualify for the loan, the borrower also must demonstrate a consistent pattern of accumulating assets. Assets may be applied toward a down payment, which lowers the lender's risk, or retained as a cushion for unexpected future expenses, which also minimizes the lender's risk.

At the very minimum, the borrower must have sufficient assets to pay for the cash down payment, any prepaid items and the closing costs of the loan. However, lenders also want the borrower to have liquid assets remaining in an amount equal to at least two month's mortgage payments after settlement.

Conventional loans require a minimum 5% down payment. Private mortgage insurance (PMI) is usually required on down payments of less than 20%. PMI protects the lender against financial loss in case the borrower defaults. Borrowers who have smaller down payments may be able to get assistance through the FHA or VA loan programs.

LIABILITIES

In assessing the degree of financial risk, lenders also consider the borrower's installment debt, revolving charge account balances, and amount of child support, alimony or maintenance payments, and any checking account credit lines.

THE PROPERTY'S APPRAISED VALUE

When deciding whether to grant a loan, lenders also consider the property's appraised market value. Lenders use a Loan-to-Value (LTV) to calculate how much mortgage money the lender is willing to lend. Basically, the LTV is the relationship-- expressed as a percentage--between the mortgage amount and the lesser of the appraised value of the property or the sales price. The higher the LTV the more financial risk to the lender, while a lower LTV generally means less risk and more latitude in approving the loan application.

Credit Score

When determining the investment quality of a loan, lenders assign the loan with the equivalent of a grade, A paper being the highest quality loan, and D paper being the highest risk to the investor.

To help determine if a loan is an A paper or not, the federal National Mortgage Association (Fannie

Mae) and the federal Home Loan Mortgage Corporation (Freddie Mac) have established guidelines to determine the investment quality of the loan. These guidelines help lenders to make their decisions and also enable the investors that buy the securities that are backed by these mortgages to know how much risk they are taking.

An investment quality loan can be defined as a loan made to a borrower from which timely repayment can be expected and that the loan is secured by sufficient collateral in case of default. A lender uses the guidelines provided by Fannie Mae and Freddie Mac to determine if a loan is of investment quality. If the loan falls outside the guidelines, it can be considered a B, C, or D paper loan, depending upon how far outside the established guidelines a particular loan falls. A lender who is making a B, C or D paper loan is taking a higher risk since there is an increased likelihood of the loan defaulting. The lender is compensated for higher risk by charging the borrower a higher interest rate. It is important to remember that the loan decision process can be subjective and the guidelines are just that, guidelines, not rules etched in stone. Therefore, different lenders may rate the same loan differently when determining the investment quality of a loan. That is where your mortgage broker comes in as he or she knows which lender can give the highest grade to your loan.

Also, some lenders use a credit scoring system to determine the credit risk. There are three main credit-scoring systems, namely Equifax's Beacon and TRW's FICO and Transunion's Empirica, which predicts the likelihood that an existing account or potential credit customer will become a serious credit risk. Beacon has a minimum credit score of 400 with a maximum of 844. FICO score ranges from mid 300's to high 800's. Empirica is similar to FICO and Beacon. The higher the credit score, the better the credit risk. Generally speaking, a credit score of 680 plus should put one in 'A' paper category. It must however be noted that not all lenders give the same value to a particular credit score. Besides, not all lenders use credit scoring system and even when they do they may not use it for all their loan programs. Once again, your mortgage broker is your best guide as he or she should know right away as to which lender will not only accept your credit score but will also be able to offer you the best rate in your situation.

Two main factors determine what Credit Grade you are. They are:

1. Credit
2. Debt Ratio

The interest rate a lender will charge depends on these two factors. If both the factors are great, the loan is assigned 'A" grade and therefore qualifies for the best interest rate. If even one of the factors is not up to par, the quality of the loan is downgraded to 'A-" or 'B' paper. Consequently, the interest rate goes up as the perceived risk factor increases.

'A' Paper: In plain English, A Paper refers to borrowers with excellent credit which means no late charges whatsoever for the last 7 years. Debt ratios of no more than 28/38. As usual, marginal exceptions are possible with strong compensating factors.

'B' Paper allows borrower three 30 day mortgage late charges;. Three 30 day and one 90 day installment or revolving accounts late charges during the last 24 months. Back end debt ratio to be no more than 48%. Any Bankruptcy dismissal or discharge should be over 3 years ago with reestablished credit. These are general guidelines and may vary from lender to lender. Exceptions are always possible with strong compensating factors. Besides 'A' and 'B', the mortgage industry also have 'A'-, 'B'+, 'C' and 'D' paper, too. D papers refer to what is known as hard money loans, which are mostly based on the equity in your home and not on your credit. Back end ratio could be as high as 65% but Loan to Value ratio drops to less than 65%.

Loan-to-Value Ratio (LTV) refers to the loan amount as percentage of the market value of the house. A $100,000 loan on a $200,000 house will be at 50% LTV. The higher the LTV, the more stringent the lenders become on credit and income. Under 65% LTV, most any loan can fly even if one has Credit and Debt Ratio problems. Even now, if one is an 'A' paper, one can get 100% LTV loan and in some cases even 125%.

Debt Ratio (DR) stands for income-to-debt ratio. Traditionally, the debt ratio has been somewhat like 28/36. 28 is called the front ratio and 36 the back ratio. They are also known as top and bottom ratios. The 28% refers to your monthly housing expense (PITI) as a percentage of your gross monthly income and 36% represents your PITI plus total of your all other recurring monthly payments on personal loans, credit cards, auto loans etc. However, lately these ratios have been stretched. FHA accepts as much as 29/41. Conventional 'A' paper loans are being done at as much as 36/42 and even more. 'D' papers loans, of-course, go up to 65% back ratio.

Besides, Credit and Debt Ratio, other factors are your discretionary income, job stability and the most important your real property also has to qualify.

FICO Score - a Brief Explanation

When you apply for a mortgage loan, you expect your lender to pull a credit report and look at whether you've made your payments on time. What you may not expect is that they seem to be more interested in your "FICO" score.

"What's a FICO score?" is a common reaction.

Each time your credit report is pulled, it is run through a computer program with a built-in scorecard. Points are awarded or deducted based on certain items such as how long you have had credit cards, whether you make your payments on time, if your credit balances are near maximum, and assorted other variables. When the credit report prints in your lenders office, the total score is displayed. Your score can be anywhere between the high 300s and the low 800s.

Lenders wanted to determine if there was any relationship between these credit scores and whether borrowers made their payments on time, so they did a study. The study showed that borrowers with scores above 680 almost always made their payments on time. Borrowers with scores below 600 seemed fairly certain to develop problems.

As a result, credit scoring became a more important factor in approving mortgage loans. Credit scores also made it easier to develop artificial intelligence computer programs that could make a "yes" decision for loans that should obviously be approved. Nowadays, a computer and not a person may have actually approved your mortgage.

In short, lower credit scores require a more thorough review than higher scores. Often, mortgage lenders will not even consider a score below 600.

Keith Startz

Some of the things that affect your FICO score are:

Delinquencies
Too many accounts opened within the last twelve months
Short credit history
Balances on revolving credit are near the maximum limits
Public records, such as tax liens, judgments, or bankruptcies
No recent credit card balances
Too many recent credit inquiries
Too few revolving accounts
Too many revolving accounts

FICO actually stands for Fair Isaac and Company, which is the company used by the Experian (formerly TRW) credit bureau to calculate credit scores. Trans-Union and Equifax are two other credit bureaus who also provide credit scores.

FICO Scores and Your Mortgage

Four years ago, credit scoring had little to do with mortgage lending. When reviewing the credit worthiness of a borrower, an underwriter would make a subjective decision based on past payment history.

Then things changed.
Lenders studied the relationship between credit scores and mortgage delinquencies. There was a definite relationship. Almost half of those

borrowers with FICO scores below 550 became ninety days delinquent at least once during their mortgage. On the other hand, only two out of every 10,000 borrowers with FICO scores above eight hundred became delinquent.

So lenders began to take a closer look at FICO scores and this is what they found out. The chart below shows the likelihood of a ninety-day delinquency for specific FICO scores.

FICO Score	Odds of a delinquent account		
595	2.25	to	1
600	4.5	to	1
615	9	to	1
630	18	to	1
645	36	to	1
660	72	to	1
680	144	to	1
700	288	to	1
780	576	to	1

If you were lending thousands of dollars, whom would you want to lend it to?

FICO Scores, What Affects Them, How Lenders Look At Them

Imagine a busy lending office and a loan officer has just ordered a credit report. He hears the whir of the laser printer and he knows the pages of the credit report are going to start spitting out in just a second. There is a moment of tension in the air. He watches the pages stack up in the collection tray, but he waits to pick them up until all of the pages are finished printing. He waits because FICO scores are located at the end of the report. Previously, he would have probably picked them up as they came off. A FICO above 700 will evoke a smile, then a grin, perhaps a shout and a "victory" style arm pump in the air. A score below 600 will definitely result in a frown, a furrowed brow, and concern.

FICO stands for Fair Isaac & Company, and credit scores are reported by each of the three major credit bureaus: TRW (Experian), Equifax, and Trans-Union. The score does not come up exactly the same on each bureau because each bureau places a slightly different emphasis on different items. Scores range from 365 to 840.

Some of the things that affect your FICO scores:

Delinquencies
Too many accounts opened within the last twelve months
Short credit history
Balances on revolving credit are near the maximum limits
Public records, such as tax liens, judgments, or bankruptcies

No recent credit card balances
Too many recent credit inquiries
Too few revolving accounts
Too many revolving accounts

Sounds confusing, doesn't it?

The credit score is actually calculated using a "scorecard" where you receive points for certain things. Creditors and lenders who view your credit report do not get to see the scorecard, so they do not know exactly how your score was calculated. They just see the final scores.

Basic guidelines on how to view the FICO scores vary a little from lender to lender. Usually, a score above 680 will require a very basic review of the entire loan package. Scores between 640 and 680 require more thorough underwriting. Once a score gets below 640, an underwriter will look at a loan application with a more cautious approach. Many lenders will not even consider a loan with a FICO score below 600, some as high as 620.

FICO Scores and Interest Rates

Credit scores can affect more than whether your loan gets approved or not. They can also affect how much you pay for your loan, too. Some lenders establish a "base price" and will reduce the points on a loan if the credit score is above a certain level. For example, one major national lender reduces the cost of a loan by a quarter point if the FICO score is greater than 725. If it is between 700 and 724, they will reduce the cost by one-eighth of a point. A point is equal to one percent of the loan amount.

There are other lenders who do it in reverse. They establish their base price, but instead of reducing the cost for good FICO scores, they "add on" costs for lower FICO scores. The results from either method would work out to be approximately the same interest rate. It is just that the second way "looks" better when you are quoting interest rates on a rate sheet or in an advertisement.

FICO Scores and Mortgage Underwriting Decisions
FICO scores are only "guidelines" and factors other than FICO scores affect underwriting decisions. Some examples of compensating factors that will make an underwriter more lenient toward lower FICO scores can be a larger down payment, low debt-to-income ratios, an excellent history of saving money, and others. There also may be a reasonable explanation for items on the credit history which negatively impact your credit score.

They Don't Always Make Sense
Even so, sometimes credit scores do not seem to make any sense at all. One borrower with a completely flawless credit history had a FICO score below 600. One borrower with a foreclosure on her credit report had a FICO above 780.

Portfolio & Sub-Prime Lenders
Finally, there are a few "portfolio" lenders who do not even look at credit scoring, at least on their

portfolio loans. A portfolio lender is usually a savings & loan institution who originates some adjustable rate mortgages that they intend to keep in their own portfolio instead of selling them in the secondary mortgage market. They may look at home loans differently. Some concentrate on the value of the home. Some may concentrate more on the savings history of the borrower. There are also "sub-prime" lenders, or "B & C paper" lenders, who will provide a home loan, but at a higher interest rate and cost.

Running Credit Reports
One thing to remember when you are shopping for a home loan is that you should not let numerous mortgage lenders run credit reports on you. Wait until you have a reasonable expectation that they are the lender you are going to use to obtain your home loan. Not only will you have to explain any credit inquiries in the last ninety days, but numerous inquiries will lower your FICO score by a small amount. This may not matter if your FICO is 780, but it would matter to you if it were 642.

Don't Buy A Car Just Before Looking for a Home!
In conclusion, a word of advice not directly related to FICO scores. When people begin to think about the possibility of buying a home, they often think about buying other big-ticket items, such as cars. Quite often when someone asks a lender to prequalify them for a home loan there is a brand new car payment on the credit report. Often, they

Keith Startz

would have qualified in their anticipated price range except that the new car payment has raised their debt-to-income ratio, lowering their maximum purchase price. Sometimes they have bought the car so recently that the new loan doesn't even show up on the credit report yet, but with six to eight credit inquiries from car dealers and automobile finance companies it is kind of obvious. Almost every time you sit down in a car dealership, it generates two inquiries into your credit.

Credit History is Important

Nowadays, credit scores are important if you want to get the best interest rate available. Protect your FICO score. Do not open new revolving accounts needlessly. Do not fill out credit applications needlessly. Do not keep your credit cards nearly maxed out. Make sure you do use your credit occasionally. Always make sure every creditor has their payment in their office no later than 29 days past due.

And never ever be more than thirty days late on your mortgage.

Cleaning up Your Credit

Mortgage lenders generally check with three credit bureaus in order to evaluate you're past payment history. Your goal in cleaning up your credit report should be to clean up each of the three bureaus. If you only work on one, this does not affect the reporting to the other bureaus.

Get a Copy of Your Credit Report

The first step is to get a copy of your merged credit report, which shows all three of the major bureaus, Experian (formerly TRW), Equifax (formerly CBI), and Trans-Union. Most mortgage lenders will obtain data from all three of these bureaus in analyzing your credit history. The exception is that some portfolio lenders (usually adjustable rate lenders) may only review one.

What to Say When You Call Your Creditors
There are two efforts that must be made. First, call any creditors reporting a negative and ask them to remove the negative item. Ask in a nice calm voice and do not get upset when they say no. Simply repeat your request over and over in your nice pleasant voice. If you get nowhere, then ask to speak to the supervisor. Make sure you keep a log of your conversation, noting the date, time, who you spoke to and what they said. Repeat this procedure over and over. In a high percentage of cases, it works.

Get Written Confirmation of Agreements
Be sure to ask for a letter by mail or fax that shows the creditor is correcting the negative information. You may need this letter for two reasons. First, they may not actually make the changes. With the letter, you can appeal directly to the credit bureau and they will make the correction. Second, if you are applying for a mortgage before the changes actually hit the credit bureaus report; your lender will need this documentation.

Keith Startz

If you have a charge off or collection account that shows as unpaid, don't just send them a check and pay it off. Call the creditor on the phone, explain that you have the funds to pay the account in full, and calmly explain why it should not have been reported on your credit in the first place. Then ask if they will provide you a letter deleting the account entirely from all credit bureaus if you pay off the account. Try to get them to fax it to you. As before, be sure to document all of your telephone contact and always keep a nice pleasant tone in your voice. In a large percentage of cases, this also works.

Disputing the Report -- When Your Creditor Will Not Remove an Item

There will be cases when the creditor does not agree to remove the negative credit item. If it is an item that is definitely not yours, call the credit bureau immediately (except for Equifax, who only responds by mail). When on the telephone, do not discuss any negative items that are accurate. Do not discuss any items that may be accurate in general but have some small error in detail that you can dispute by mail. Once you confirm any accuracy at all, you cannot dispute it later by mail.

For the remaining items, you need to dispute them by mail, writing directly to the credit bureaus. Write a letter to the appropriate bureau including your name, social security number, address, disputed accounts, and account numbers. You must sign the letter. Inform the bureau that you are disputing the data as it appears on your credit report.

Mistakes on Your Credit Report

Almost every item on your credit report will have some mistake, even if only slight. Do not acknowledge any of the accuracies, but be sure to note all inaccuracies. Write next to each item something like, "not mine, not accurate, mistaken item, complete error," or whatever is most appropriate. Request a copy of the corrected report within thirty days. If they do not respond within 30 days, send another letter. In this letter you will include a copy of your dated original letter and a new letter firmly requesting they remove the disputed information. Include a cc: to the Federal Trade Commission.

Do Not Call the Credit Bureaus - Write Letters

The credit bureau may write a letter asking you to call. Do not call under any circumstances. Your phone call will be recorded and a log will be made of the conversation. Simply write back with copies of your original letters, telling them of the original date you submitted your request. Keep a file of all correspondence to and from the credit bureau and follow through continually. Do not get discouraged, as this will be worth your while.

What happens is that the credit bureaus forward your dispute to the individual creditors. Who have forty-five days to respond? If they do not respond within the allotted time the item must be removed. However, if they do respond at a later date with information that documents the credit report is correct, the item will be placed back on your credit report.

Bankruptcies

For those of you who have filed bankruptcy in the past, the items that were discharged will normally show up as a charge-off or uncollected debt. You will want to write to the credit bureaus, providing a copy of your complete bankruptcy papers and request that they show the debt as "discharged in bankruptcy." This looks better and raises your FICO score. FICO sores above 680 make it easier to obtain mortgage loans.

14657495R00038

Made in the USA
Lexington, KY
14 April 2012